Lewis and Clark

written and illustrated by
Rod Espinosa

visit us at
www.abdopublishing.com

Published by Magic Wagon, a division of the ABDO Publishing Group, 8000 West 78th Street, Edina, Minnesota 55439. Copyright © 2008 by Abdo Consulting Group, Inc. International copyrights reserved in all countries. All rights reserved. No part of this book may be reproduced in any form without written permission from the publisher. Graphic Planet™ is a trademark and logo of Magic Wagon.

Printed in the United States.

Written and illustrated by Rod Espinosa
Colored and lettered by Rod Espinosa
Edited by Stephanie Hedlund
Interior layout and design by Antarctic Press
Cover art by Rod Espinosa
Cover design by Neil Klinepier

Library of Congress Cataloging-in-Publication Data

Espinosa, Rod.
    Lewis and Clark / written and illustrated by Rod Espinosa.
    p. cm. -- (Bio-graphics)
    Includes index.
    ISBN 978-1-60270-069-7
    1. Lewis and Clark Expedition (1804-1806)--Juvenile literature. 2. West (U.S.)--Discovery and exploration--Juvenile literature. 3. West (U.S.)--Description and travel--Juvenile literature. 4. Lewis, Meriwether, 1774-1809--Juvenile literature. 5. Clark, William, 1770-1838--Juvenile literature. 6. Explorers--West (U.S.)--Biography--Juvenile literature. 7. Graphic novels. I. Title.

F592.7.E77 2008
 917.804'2--dc22

                                                        2007005578

TABLE of CONTENTS

Washington D.C., June 20, 1803 To Meriwether Lewis esquire, Captain of the 1st regiment of infantry of the United States of America.

The object of your mission is to explore the Missouri river, & such principal stream of it as by it's course and communication with the waters of the Pacific ocean whether the Columbia, Oregon, Colorado or any other river may offer the most direct & practicable water communication across this continent for the purpose of commerce.

President Thomas Jefferson

With those words, President Thomas Jefferson sent his good friend Meriwether Lewis to lead an expedition into unexplored territory!

Meriwether Lewis was an adventurer at heart. To prepare for this momentous trip, he took courses in medicine, botany, zoology, and celestial navigation.

Lewis chose as his second in command, an ex-lieutenant named William Clark. Clark was a skillful mapmaker and an experienced river navigator.

He studied many maps and everything that was known by traders and explorers before him.

A rugged frontiersman, Clark was the perfect choice. He would share command with Lewis.

Lewis and Clark assembled a team of men to accompany them on their momentous journey. The group was made up of soldiers, expert hunters, and frontiersmen. They were known as the Corps of Discovery.

Clark had a 55-foot-long keelboat constructed for the journey. The Corps of Discovery set sail on Monday, May 14, 1804.

The group sailed, rowed, pulled, and pushed their craft among the many hazards of spring runoff on the Mississippi River. The Corps of Discovery quickly became a good team under the leadership of Lewis and Clark.

Soon after, they lost crew member Charles Floyd to illness. They worried about losing more men along the way.

IT'S RAINING EVEN HARDER! LET'S PUT TO SHORE.

On May 25, they passed by La Charette, the last settlement on the Missouri. Forty-three men ventured into the unknown.

WE ARE LARGELY ON OUR OWN NOW...

WE'LL BE DEPENDING ON EACH OTHER FROM NOW ON.

August 1804. The Corps of Discovery met with the Native American tribes, the Otos and the Missouris.

WE COME IN PEACE AND BRING GREETINGS FROM OUR CHIEF, THOMAS JEFFERSON. THE UNITED STATES OF AMERICA WILL PROTECT YOU IF YOU TRADE WITH US.

WE NEED PROTECTION FROM THE TETON SIOUX. WE WILL TRADE WITH YOUR NATION.

October 1804. North Dakota. At a friendly Mandan village, the explorers settled down to winter quarters. They would not move again until spring.

This gave the leaders an opportunity to make plans for the journey ahead.

WE WON'T BE ABLE TO USE THE KEELBOAT NORTH. THE RIVER IS TOO SHALLOW.

WE CAN SEND IT BACK TO ST. LOUIS WITH THE MAPS AND NOTES WE'VE MADE SO FAR.

SIR! WE MET A FRENCHMAN WHO SAYS HE KNOWS MANY INDIAN LANGUAGES.

On November 4, a trader named Toussaint Charbonneau offered his services as an interpreter. With him was his Shoshone wife.

MONSIEUR, I OFFER MY SERVICES AS AN INTERPRETER. MY WIFE SPEAKS HIDATSA AND SHOSHONE.

WE ARE CERTAIN TO MEET HER TRIBE IF YOU ARE GOING WEST.

EXCELLENT. WHAT IS HER NAME?

SACAGAWEA, MONSIEUR.

At Fort Mandan on Tuesday, February 11, 1805, Sacagawea gave birth to a son.

WELL, I'LL BE...

I HEARD THE INDIANS SAY IT'S A GOOD SIGN.

The baby was named Jean Baptiste Charbonneau. The men of the Corps of Discovery nicknamed him "Pompy."

In March 1805, the ice on the Missouri River broke up. The Corps of Discovery sent a group back to St. Louis.

WE'LL SEE YOU BACK IN ST. LOUIS, SERGEANT. BRING THOSE SPECIMENS, MAPS, AND LETTERS TO OUR PRESIDENT.

AYE, SIR!

I WOULD HAVE LIKED TO KEEP OUR LARGE KEELBOAT.

WE'RE ABOUT TO PENETRATE A COUNTRY AT LEAST 2,000 MILES IN WIDTH.

INDEED. LET US PRESS ON!

The rest of the group continued on. The journey northwards amazed them all.

LOOK AT ALL THOSE BIRDS! THEY'RE EVERYWHERE!

WE'RE NOT GOING HUNGRY HERE, THAT'S FOR SURE.

Chapter 3 Into the Wilderness

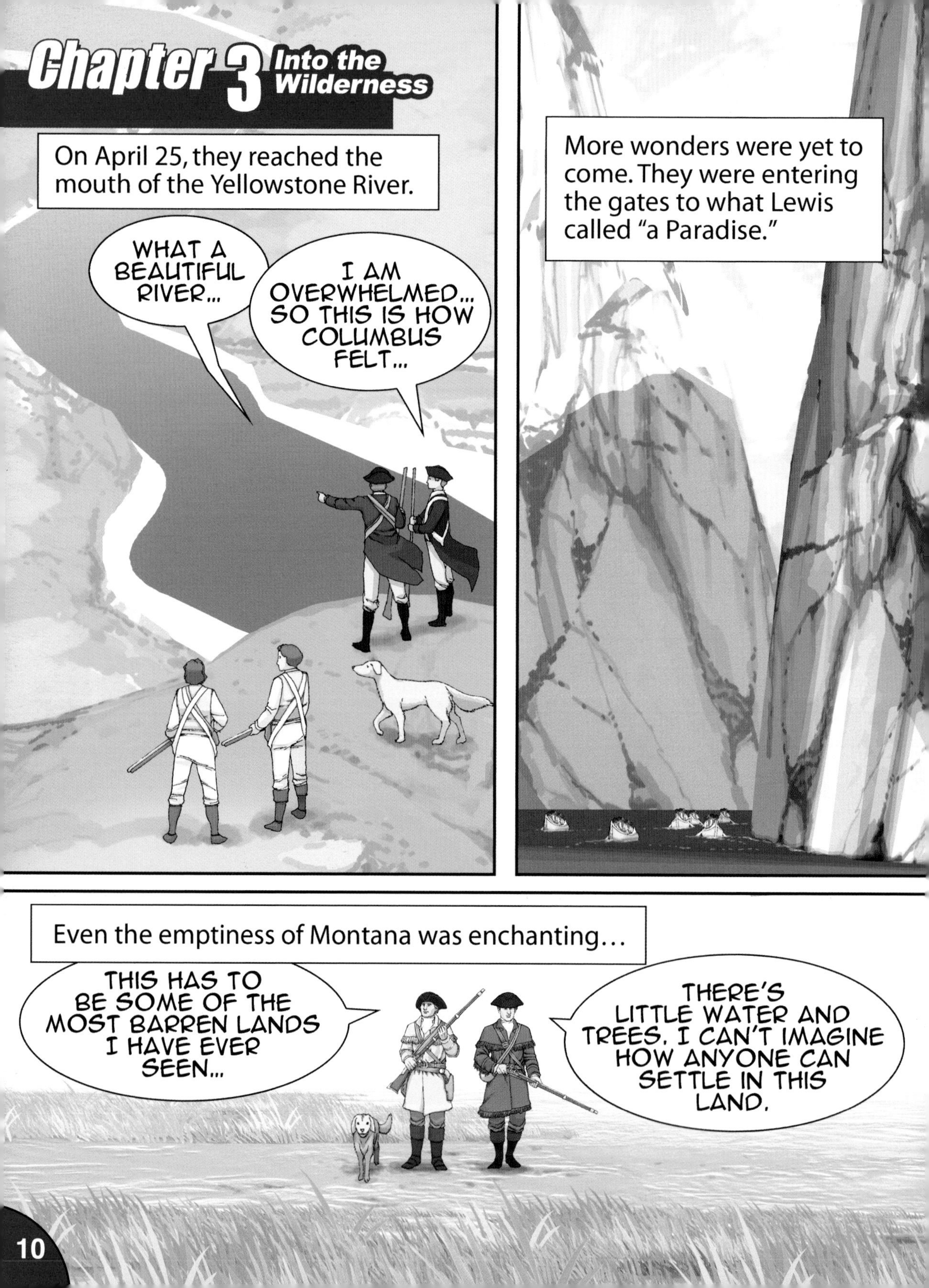
On April 25, they reached the mouth of the Yellowstone River.
WHAT A BEAUTIFUL RIVER...
I AM OVERWHELMED... SO THIS IS HOW COLUMBUS FELT...
More wonders were yet to come. They were entering the gates to what Lewis called "a Paradise."
Even the emptiness of Montana was enchanting…
THIS HAS TO BE SOME OF THE MOST BARREN LANDS I HAVE EVER SEEN...
THERE'S LITTLE WATER AND TREES. I CAN'T IMAGINE HOW ANYONE CAN SETTLE IN THIS LAND.

There was also danger! For when night came, wolves and other hunting beasts came out!

THEY'RE LARGER THAN ANY DOG I HAVE EVER SEEN!

KEEP THE FIRE GOING!

In June 1805, the Corps of Discovery came upon a fork in the river…

THE TRIBESMEN WE TALKED TO NEVER SAID ANYTHING ABOUT A FORK IN THE RIVER.

WHICH ONE IS THE MISSOURI?

I WILL GO EXPLORE THIS BRANCH.

While Lewis explored the north fork of the river, Clark led the rest of the group along the west fork. It was at this time that Sacagawea fell ill.

LEWIS SHOULD BE COMING BACK ANYTIME NOW. I'VE DONE MY BEST TO HEAL HER...

After a few tense days, she slowly recovered.

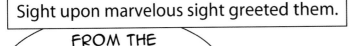

Sight upon marvelous sight greeted them.

FROM THE COMMENCEMENT OF TIME, ALL SUCH BEAUTY HAS BEEN CONCEALED FROM THE EYES OF CIVILIZED MAN...

... OR FROM HIS STOMACH. LET'S ROAST SOME.

Clark chose the right river. After going 45 miles up the Missouri, Clark was sure he was still on the Missouri when it pointed south straight into the Rocky Mountains. Lewis went 80 miles north before turning back.

THE RIVER I WAS ON WASN'T THE RIGHT ONE. I'LL NAME IT MARIA'S RIVER AFTER MY COUSIN.

LOOK! A WALL LIES BEFORE US!

CAN THE BOUNDLESS MISSOURI END THERE, PERHAPS?

THOSE ARE VERY ROCKY MOUNTAINS...

They traveled overland, carrying their canoes. The Corps of Discovery arrived at the Missouri Falls on June 13, 1805.

MY INITIAL ESTIMATE OF A ONE-DAY PORTAGE MAY BE MISTAKEN.

THESE FALLS MAY BE LARGER THAN WE THOUGHT.

CHARBONNEAU, WHAT IS SHE DOING?

SHE IS DIGGING FOR ROOTS, MONSIEUR.

Sacagawea's gathering of roots and berries along the way helped feed the entire camp.

MONSIEUR, MY WIFE SAYS HER TRIBE LIVES BEYOND THESE FALLS. IF WE CAN REACH THEM BEFORE WINTER COMES, THEY WILL HELP US.

In the end, the portage route they took around the falls was 18 miles long!

They hoped to find the Shoshone tribe before winter fully set in.

I DON'T UNDERSTAND. THE SHOSHONE SHOULD BE HERE.

WE NEED TO FIND THEM SOON.

YES, BEFORE WINTER SETS IN.

The Rocky Mountains proved to be very difficult to cross.

The higher they went, the colder it got.

While it was still sunny down in the valleys, the hills were thick with snow.

DON'T WORRY. SGT. DROUILLARD IS A GOOD HUNTER.

THEY SHOULD BE BACK WITH SOME FOOD SOON.

Still, the Corps of Discovery marched on. Under the captains' leadership, they remained cheerful and upbeat.

Lewis went ahead of the group. He continued up the Beaverhead River and reached the Continental Divide on August 12.

THANK GOD I HAVE LIVED TO BESTRIDE THE MIGHTY AND HERETOFORE DEEMED ENDLESS MISSOURI!

INDEED, SGT. MCNEAL.

SWEET IS THE WATER THAT FLOWS FROM THE MOST DISTANT FOUNTAIN THAT SUPPLIES IT.

With time running out, the Corps of Discovery depended on Sacagawea's memories of her homeland.

Suddenly, the people they were looking for appeared!

QUICK, GEORGE, TELL THEM WE COME IN PEACE!

FEAR NOT. WE COME IN PEACE.

THERE! THAT RIVER LEADS TO MY PEOPLE. I AM ALMOST HOME!

There was a reunion between Sacagewea and her brother Cameahwait. It was a tearful reunion with lots of rejoicing. The tribespeople looked over the group, marveling at their appearance and even their dog.

19

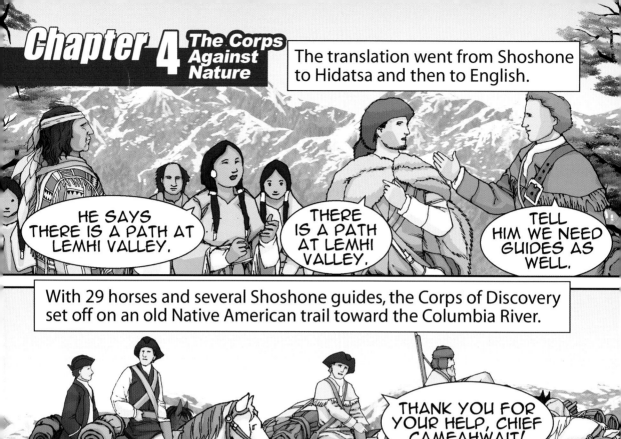

The translation went from Shoshone to Hidatsa and then to English.

HE SAYS THERE IS A PATH AT LEMHI VALLEY.

THERE IS A PATH AT LEMHI VALLEY.

TELL HIM WE NEED GUIDES AS WELL.

With 29 horses and several Shoshone guides, the Corps of Discovery set off on an old Native American trail toward the Columbia River.

THANK YOU FOR YOUR HELP, CHIEF CAMEAHWAIT!

The trail proved difficult and dangerous!

LOOK OUT THERE!

THE MEN ARE GETTING WEAK FROM HUNGER.

The 11 days across the Bitterroot Mountains to the Clearwater River were the hardest part of their trip.

WE'VE GOT TO GET OUT OF THIS WEATHER!

THAT'S A BRILLIANT SUGGESTION, MY GOOD FRIEND!

Bitter cold, dense forests, and the lack of game animals combined to make the journey a difficult one. Many of the group became sick for lack of food and exposure to cold.

SACAGAWEA, TAKE MY RATION. I'M STILL FULL.

MERCI, MONSIEUR.

The weather was not the only danger they had to face!

GOOD GOD! THAT CREATURE IS TALLER THAN TWO MEN!

STEADY, MEN!

Luckily, they reached the Weippe Prairie, where they met the Nez Perce. The Nez Perce were very friendly and shared their food with them.

I THINK THEIR DRIED FISH DOES NOT AGREE WITH ME...

THEIR MEDICINE MAN IS OFFERING TO DRIVE AWAY EVIL SPIRITS FROM YOUR BODY.

Bidding their Nez Perce friends farewell, the Corps of Discovery marched onward!

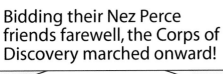

WITH THE ROCKY MOUNTAINS BEHIND US, THE WAY IS OPEN TO THE COLUMBIA RIVER.

LET US PRESS ON!

They navigated the rapids of the Snake River. The roughest of the rapids was the 55-mile-long stretch that began with the 38-foot Celilo Falls. And then it was on to the Dalles.

HOLD ON, MEN! WE'RE ALMOST THERE!

Finally, their goal came in sight... the Pacific Ocean!

WE'RE FINALLY HERE...

I'M GLAD WE MADE IT!

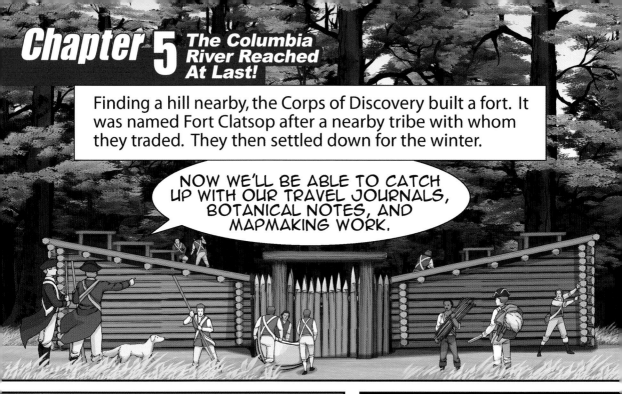

Finding a hill nearby, the Corps of Discovery built a fort. It was named Fort Clatsop after a nearby tribe with whom they traded. They then settled down for the winter.

NOW WE'LL BE ABLE TO CATCH UP WITH OUR TRAVEL JOURNALS, BOTANICAL NOTES, AND MAPMAKING WORK.

They also talked and traded with the natives.

WHAT? WE PAID ALL THOSE BEADS FOR THIS?

On New Year's Day, the group celebrated by firing their muskets in the air and eating boiled elk.

WE TRAVELED 4,132 MILES IN 554 DAYS, FROM THE WOOD RIVER TO THE MOUTH OF THE COLUMBIA.

I'M LOOKING FORWARD TO FEASTING WITH JEFFERSON AROUND THIS TIME NEXT YEAR...

From December 7 to March 23, the Corps of Discovery lived comfortably in Fort Clatsop. They had discovered many new places and had seen many astounding things. Now, it was time to go back home.

IF WE MAKE GOOD TIME, WE MAY BE ABLE TO REACH THE NATIVE SETTLEMENTS. WHAT WERE THEIR NAMES?

WANAPAMS OR THE TENINOS. WE CAN TRADE THESE CANOES IN FOR HORSES AND FOOD.

On March 23, 1806, the Corps of Discovery started back up the Columbia.

By the end of April, the Corps of Discovery traded their canoes for horses.

WAHKIAKUMS, WATLALAS, WISHRAMS, MULTNOMAHS, UMATILLAS, KATHLAMETS, TENINOS...TARNATION! THEY ALL DRIVE A HARD BARGAIN!

WE MIGHT RUN OUT OF MONEY AT THIS RATE.

At the villages of the Walulas and the Yakamas, Lewis and Clark were welcomed. The Walula chief Yelleppit held a banquet in their honor.

THIS IS MUCH BETTER. I WONDER WHAT SHE SAID THAT MADE THE CHIEF SO HAPPY TO SEE US?

I'M SURE IT'S NOT YOUR DULL SPEECH ABOUT THE GREAT EMPIRE OF CHIEF THOMAS JEFFERSON...

25

Clark's group explored the Yellowstone River. He had a party of 23 including Charbonneau, Sacagawea and her little son.

After the Nez Perce helped them cross the Rockies, the group split to explore two routes.

Lewis took an overland route to the falls.

They planned to meet where the Missouri and Yellowstone rivers met.

Captain Lewis explored Hellgate Canyon and the Continental Divide. They soon ran into some Blackfoot tribesmen, whom the Nez Perce feared!

I THINK I SAID THE WRONG THING WHEN I TOLD THEM WE WERE FRIENDS OF THE SHOSHONE AND THE NEZ PERCE!

I AGREE, CAPTAIN!

After two years of adventure, the Corps of Discovery arrived back at Fort Mandan on August 17. There, they bade farewell to Charbonneau, Sacagawea, and their son, Jean Baptiste.

WHEN HE IS OLD ENOUGH, I WOULD LIKE TO TAKE JEAN BACK EAST. HE WILL BE EDUCATED IN THE BEST SCHOOLS.

THANK YOU FOR YOUR GENEROUS OFFER, MONSIEUR CLARK.

On September 21, the Corps of Discovery landed in St. Charles. There, they were greeted by crowds of people. Two days later, they were welcomed back to St. Louis.

Lewis and Clark were congratulated by the president. There was so much to share about their expedition.

In 1814, Clark published a two-volume account of their expedition. Many other books would be written about their successful voyage and contribution to expanding the United States.

27

Timeline

1770 - William Clark was born on August 1 in Caroline County, Virginia.

1774 - Meriwether Lewis was born on August 28 near Charlottesville, Virginia.

Spring 1803 - President Thomas Jefferson commissioned an expedition to explore the United States. Meriwether Lewis was chosen as commander.

Summer 1803 - A large keelboat was built, and William Clark and other crew members were gathered.

May 14, 1804 - The expedition began.

October 24, 1804 - The expedition stopped for the winter at Fort Mandan.

November 4, 1804 - French Canadian Toussaint Charbonneau and his wife, Sacagawea, were hired as interpreters.

February 11, 1805 - Sacagawea gave birth to son named Jean Baptiste.

June 13, 1805 - Lewis came across the Great Falls of the Missouri.

October 18, 1805 - The expedition reached the Columbia River.

November 7, 1805 - Clark made his famous journal entry, "Ocean in view! O! The joy!"

September 23, 1806 - Lewis and Clark returned to St. Louis.

October 11, 1809 - Meriwether Lewis died.

September 1, 1838 - William Clark died.

LEWIS AND CLARK'S EXPEDITION ROUTE

Further Reading

Ditchfield, Christin. *The Lewis and Clark Expedition.* A True Book. New York: Scholastic Press, 2006.

Hamilton, John. *Corps of Discovery.* Lewis & Clark Expedition. Edina: ABDO Publishing Company, 2003.

Marcovitz, Hal. *Sacagawea: Guide for the Lewis and Clark Expedition.* New York: Facts on File, 2000.

Petrie, Kristin. *Lewis and Clark.* Explorers. Edina: ABDO Publishing Company, 2007.

Glossary

barren - growing little or no crops, grasses, or plants.

botany - a branch of the science of biology that focuses on plant life.

celestial - of or relating to the sky and the visible elements of it such as the sun, moon, and stars.

Continental Divide - the line of highest points of North America. These ranges separate the waters flowing west from those flowing north or east.

keelboat - a shallow, covered riverboat that is usually rowed, poled, or towed. A keelboat is used to carry cargo.

portage - the transporting of boats or goods across land from one body of water to another.

zoology - a branch of the science of biology that focuses on animal life.

Web Sites

To learn more about Lewis and Clark, visit ABDO Publishing Company on the World Wide Web at **www.abdopublishing.com.** Web sites about Lewis and Clark are featured on our Book Links page. These links are routinely monitored and updated to provide the most current information available.

Index